# Sincerely, Emerson

## A Girl, Her Letter, and the Helpers All Around Us

by EMERSON WEBER    illustrated by JACLYN SINQUETT

HARPER
*An Imprint of HarperCollinsPublishers*

To Mom, Dad, and my brother, Finn.
To all my pen pals near and far. And,
of course, to my mailman, Doug.

—E.W.

For Rick, who makes the world
a better, brighter place.

—J.S.

Library of Congress Control Number: 2020943160
ISBN 978-0-06-306696-0

The artist used watercolor, colored pencils, and digital painting
to create the illustrations for this book.
Hand lettering by Jaclyn Sinquett
Typography by Dana Fritts

20 21 22 23 24   PC   10 9 8 7 6 5 4 3 2 1
❖
First Edition

*E*merson loved writing letters.

She loved writing "Dear."
She loved writing "Sincerely."
Most of all, she loved writing everything
that came in between.

Stories. News. Questions. Em put a piece of her life into each one.

Her brother's latest games. Taylor Swift's best songs. And her favorite jokes.

Why do you never see elephants hiding in trees?

A: Because they're really good at it.

Em wasn't done with a letter until it was perfectly decorated—the envelope too!

Then she sent her letters out into the world.
To friends and family all over. Each letter was
a connection. Em's letters made a network of
hellos, a network of love.

One day, Em got to thinking. There was one person who made it all possible. How come she had never noticed him before?

His name was Doug.

Every letter that left Em's hands went straight into Doug's. He was always there—every day. No matter what, he kept Em's letters going out into the world.

And so Em decided to write Doug his own letter.

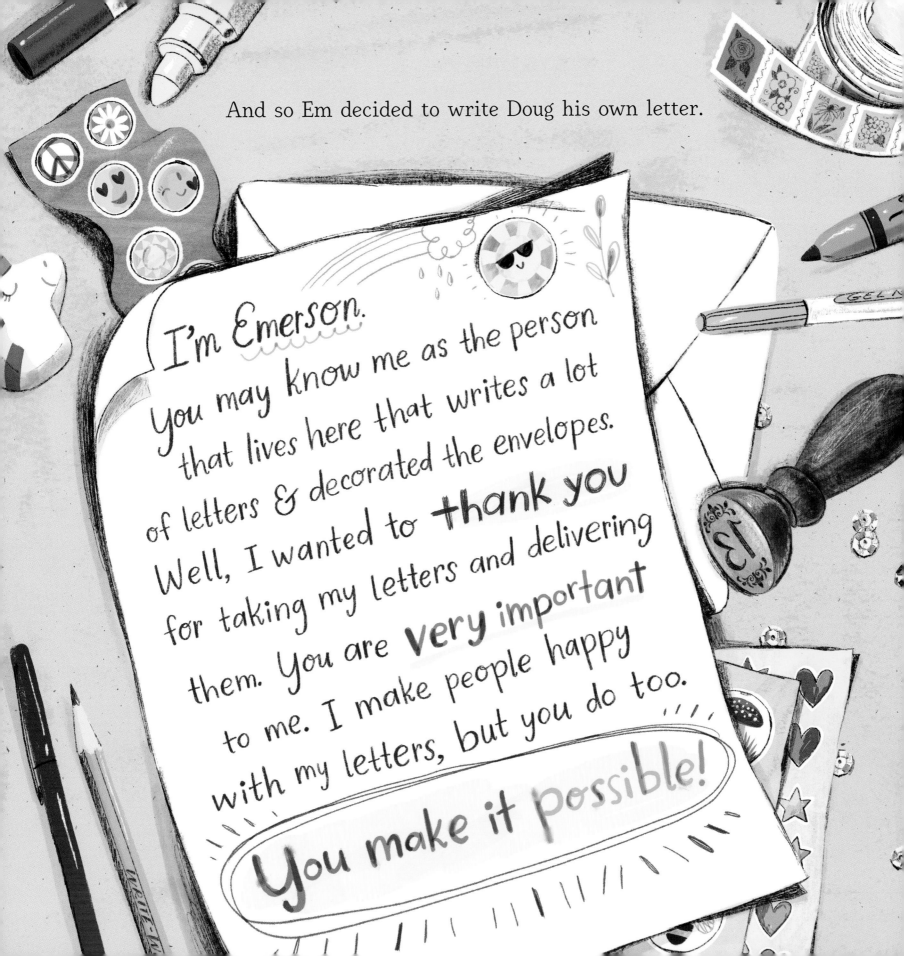

I'm Emerson. You may know me as the person that lives here that writes a lot of letters & decorated the envelopes. Well, I wanted to **thank you** for taking my letters and delivering them. You are **very** important to me. I make people happy with my letters, but you do too.

You make it possible!

She put it in the box,
and she smiled when he took it.

The next week, something remarkable happened.

Doug got out of his truck, just like he did every day. But this time, he had two whole boxes full of letters—and they were all for Emerson!

You see, Doug had told his friends at the post office all about Em's letter . . .

And they had all told their friends . . .

And soon . . .

Em's letter of thanks had reached nearly
every mail carrier in the country.

And lots and lots and lots of those
mail carriers had written her back.

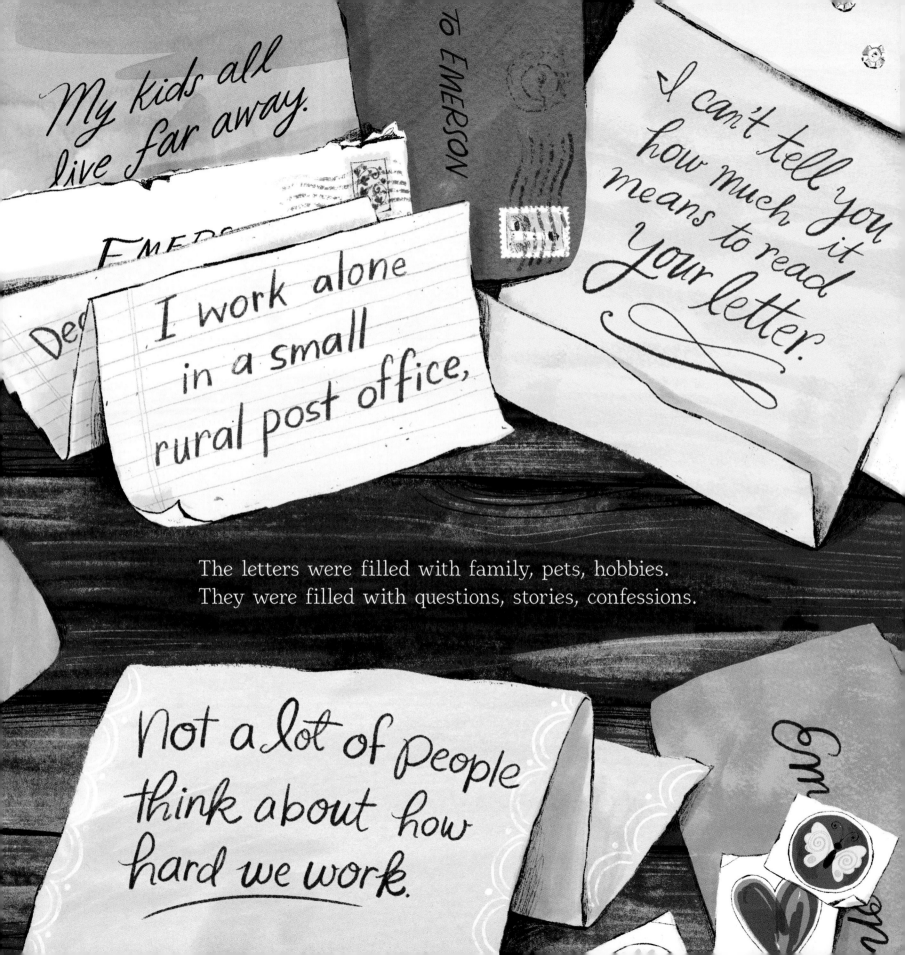

My kids all live far away.

TO EMERSON

I can't tell you how much it means to read your letter.

I work alone in a small rural post office,

The letters were filled with family, pets, hobbies.
They were filled with questions, stories, confessions.

Not a lot of people think about how hard we work.

I have a son in Kuwait, and if you have a second to send him a letter, he would love it.

They were filled with kindness.

erson

To Emer

I know you can't write back to all of us, but maybe I can drop you a line from time to time?

Every one of the letters was a connection.
Every letter had a piece of someone's life in it.

With dozens of new pen pals,
Em did what she was best at doing:
She wrote letters.

She wrote the dad.
She wrote his son.
She sent new jokes.
New stories about her life.
And she asked lots and lots of questions.

And Emerson got to thinking.

About all those people out there, living their lives. Working hard. Delivering letters. Keeping people connected. There was love in their work.

And it wasn't just the mail carriers. It was the bus drivers. The grocery store clerks. The trash collectors and the farmers. There was love in their work too.

Every day, they got up and went to work.
Every day, they did their best.

Every day, they kept the world going.
Millions and billions of people.

Every bus ride, every tomato. Every bag
of trash, every bag of groceries.

They were possible because someone cared.
Each act was an act of love . . .

. . . wrapping the world together in a network . . .

. . . like the biggest hug ever.

Emerson wished that everyone she knew
would take a moment to notice each one
of them, and thank them . . .

. . . maybe even thank each other . . . sincerely.

# Hi there!

The story you just read is 100% **true**. I know because it really happened to me! I live in South Dakota with my mom, dad, and brother, and I never expected so much to happen just because I took the time to say **thank you** to Doug, a person I saw every day.

## But it did!

I got to talk to important people, be on television, and I even got a really, really special letter from someone I admire a whole lot ("m" hi, **Taylor**). All of that made me super happy of course, but it also made me think. Why was my saying thank you such a **big deal**? Isn't saying thank you, and meaning it, something we should all be doing all the time? I think so—so I'm going to keep doing it! And I hope you will, too.

How about I start with you? **Thank you** for reading my book. I hope it made you smile, and in case it didn't, here's a joke that might do the trick—

Q: How do you catch a squirrel?
A: Climb up a tree and act like a **nut**.

Sincerely,
Emerson